Music Minus One Vocals

BROADWAY HITS
for Soprano

 2142

BROADWAY HITS
for Soprano

CONTENTS

Complete Track	Minus Track		Page
1	11	The Lusty Month Of May	4
2	12	I Could Have Danced All Night	8
3	13	Climb Every Mountain	10
4	14	Show Me	12
5	15	My Man's Gone Now	14
6	16	I Loved You Once In Silence	16
7	17	Something Wonderful	18
8	18	Summertime	20
9	19	My White Knight	21
10	20	Life Upon The Wicked Stage	23

ISBN 978-1-941566-42-8

MMO 2142

The Lusty Month Of May

from "Camelot"

**Words and Music by
Alan Jay Lerner and Frederick Loewe**

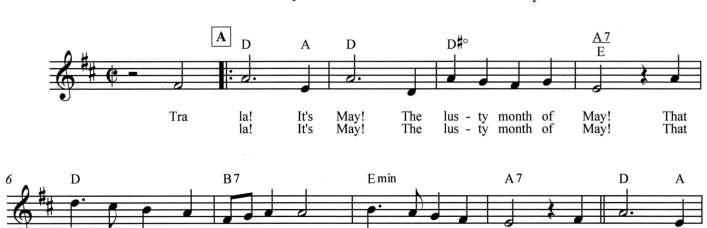

Tra la! It's May! The lus-ty month of May! That
la! It's May! The lus-ty month of May! That

love-ly month when ev-ery-one goes bliss-ful-ly a-stray. Tra la! It's
dar-ling month when ev-ery-one throws self con-trol a-way. It's time to

here! That shock-ing time of year, when tons of wick-ed lit-tle thoughts
do a wretch-ed thing or two, and try to make each pre-cious day

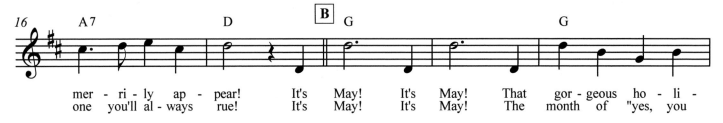

mer-ri-ly ap-pear! It's May! It's May! That gor-geous ho-li-
one you'll al-ways rue! It's May! It's May! The month of "yes, you

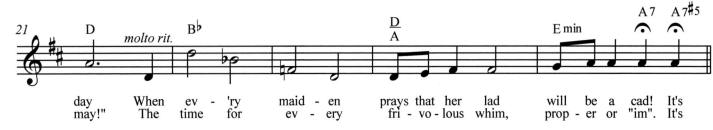

day When ev-'ry maid-en prays that her lad will be a cad! It's
may!" The time for ev-ery fri-vo-lous whim, prop-er or "im". It's

mad! It's gay! A li-bel-ous dis-play! Those drear-y vows that
wild! It's gay! A blot in ev-ery way. The birds and bees with

This page left blank to facilitate page turns.

I Could Have Danced All Night

from "My Fair Lady"

**Words and Music by
Alan Jay Lerner and Frederick Loewe**

Climb Every Mountain

from "The Sound Of Music"

**Words and Music by
Oscar Hammerstein II and
Richard Rodgers**

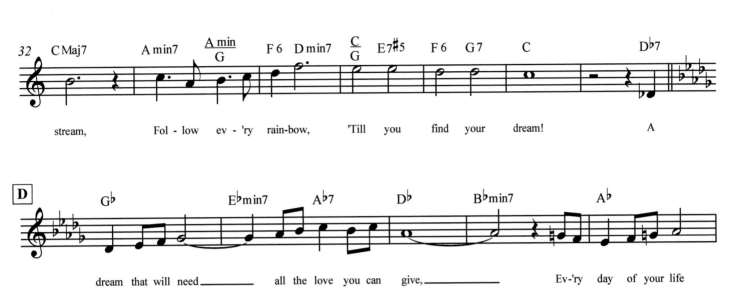

stream,   Fol - low ev - 'ry rain-bow,   'Till you find your dream!   A

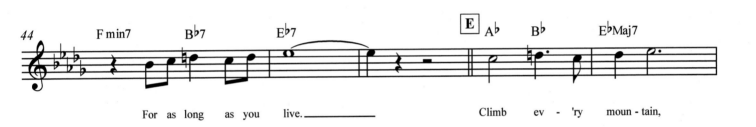

dream that will need_____ all the love you can give,_____ Ev-'ry day of your life

For as long as you live._____ Climb ev - 'ry moun - tain,

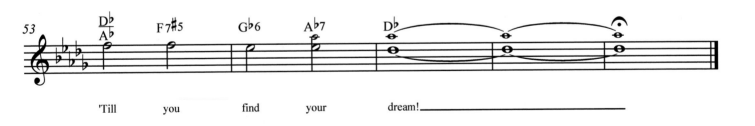

Ford ev - 'ry stream,   Fol - low ev - 'ry rain - bow,

'Till you find your dream!_____

Show Me

from "My Fair Lady"

**Words and Music by
Alan Jay Lerner and Frederick Loewe**

My Man's Gone Now

from "Porgy & Bess"

**Words and Music by
DuBose and Dorothy Heyward,
Ira Gershwin,
and George Gershwin**

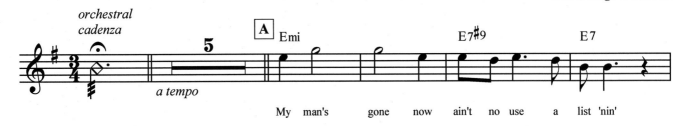

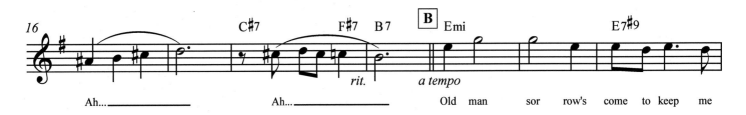

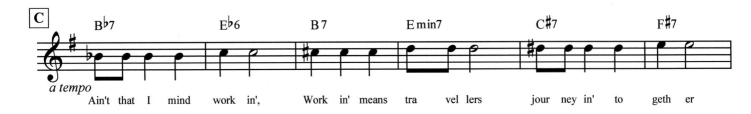

I Loved You Once In Silence

from "Camelot"

**Words and Music by
Alan Jay Lerner and Frederick Loewe**

Something Wonderful

from "The King and I"

Words and Music by
Oscar Hammerstein II and Richard Rodgers

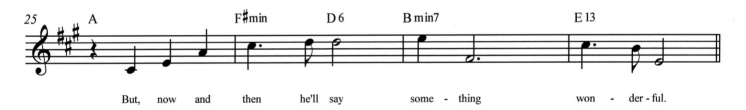

Summertime

from "Porgy and Bess"

**Words and Music by
DuBose and Dorothy Heyward,
Ira Gershwin,
and George Gershwin**

My White Knight

from "The Music Man"

Words and Music by
Meredith Willson

MMO 2142

Life Upon The Wicked Stage

from "Show Boat"

**Words and Music by
Oscar Hammerstein II and Jerome Kern**

1, 3. Life up - on the wick - ed stage ain't ev - er what a girl sup - pos - es;
2. Though you're warned a - gainst a ro - ué ru - in - ing your re - pu - ta - tion,

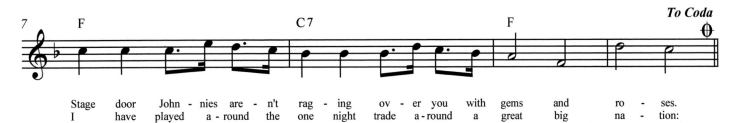

Stage door John - nies are - n't rag - ing ov - er you with gems and ro - ses.
I have played a - round the one night trade a - round a great big na - tion:

When you let a fel - ler hold your hand (which means an ex - tra beer or sand - wich),
Wild old men who give you jewels and sa - bles on - ly live in Ae - sop's Fa - bles.

Ev - 'ry - bo - dy whis - pers: "Ain't her life a whirl?"_____

Life up - on the wick - ed stage ain't noth - in' for a girl. (Though we've lis - tened to you

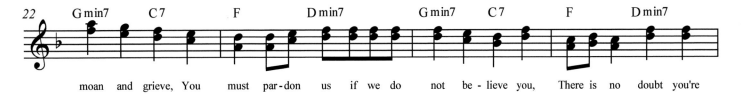

moan and grieve, You must par - don us if we do not be - lieve you, There is no doubt you're

MMO 2142

cra-zy a - bout your aw - ful stage!)   I ad-mit it's fun to smear my face with paint,

Caus-ing ev - 'ry-one to think I'm what I ain't, And I like to play a de - mi - mon - dy role with

soul!   Ask the he - ro does he like the way I lure, When I play a hus - sy or a par - a-mour?

Yet when once the cur - tain's down my life is pure, and how I dread it!

3. If some gen - tle-man would talk with rea - son, I would can - cel all next sea - son

Life up - on the wick-ed stage ain't no-thing for a girl. (You'll be back the sea - son af - ter!)

Music Minus One
50 Executive Boulevard • Elmsford, New York 10523-1325
914-592-1188 • e-mail: info@musicminusone.com
www.musicminusone.com

MMO 2142

ISBN 978-1-941566-42-8